Dying Dog Poems

poems by

Lynne Schmidt

Finishing Line Press
Georgetown, Kentucky

Dying Dog Poems

For Kyla PoopiePants

ACKNOWLEDGMENTS

Do I Just Let The Cancer Take You? was published with *34 Orchard*
Not Ready to Let Go was published by *Sheila-Na-Gig*
Still Life In A Capitalist Nightmare, Patches, and An Ode To The Now vs
Then Rescue Dog Photo were published in *The Unaccounted For Circles Of Hell*
Playtime was published in Issue 2 of *Olit*
Monstering who published On How Dogs Choose Their People
Present Moment by All Female Menu who published Kyla
The Judge was published in Volume 9 of *Frost Meadow Review*
A Field Guide For Removing Your Dead Dog's Harness was published in
Volume 10 of *Frost Meadow Review*
SAFTA Writing Residency for giving me the space to help generate the
poems, On How Dogs Choose Their People, Kyla, When He Screams
Long Enough A Local Domestic Abuse Survivor Gets Text Reading,
"Are You Safe?"

Publisher: Leah Huete de Maines
Editor: Christen Kincaid
Cover Art: Molly Blyth-Olson Illustration
Author Photo: Meaghan Martin Photography
Cover Design: Elizabeth Maines McCleavy

Order online: www.finishinglinepress.com
also available on amazon.com

Author inquiries and mail orders:
Finishing Line Press
PO Box 1626
Georgetown, Kentucky 40324
USA

Contents

The Last Will and Testament of Kyla PoopiePants

To Enyo, I leave my beds, my bowl, my leash. May you find comfort in them. Also—I'm still mad about you biting off that piece of my ear, so really, you only get sloppy seconds.

To Zoë, I leave my tennis balls. I hope someday you learn how to play with toys. It is truly the best. I also leave my life jacket, and various other clothing. I think most of them will fit you. Sorry about trying to bite you in the face.

To TaylorSwift, I leave you nothing. You shouldn't have attacked me so many times. You made the apartment a scary place… though, I suppose you may sleep on my beds once I'm gone.

To Courtney, thank you for the walkies when my human was hurt. Thank you for coming to visit after I was sick, and bringing chickie nuggies. I leave you the love you have for Ripley, especially the cuddles.

To my human's roommate, I leave meat snacks. Thank you, Mr. SausageMan, for the campfires, the Doctor Poop Song, and the sausage, ham, spam, kielbasa, jerky. Now it's all for you. May there be sausage in everything you eat.

To the future dogs my human will rescue, I leave my human. I loved her more than any squeaky ball, any meat snack. I hope you love her, too.

To my human, I leave the nine years we shared together.

I'll visit you when I can.

Patches

I met her in a Wal Mart parking lot
and fell in love as children do.
I begged and pleaded and won.
We put her tiny body in the car,
and my sister told me I was selfish and stupid.

My father chained her to a dog house in Michigan.
Said she was never allowed in the house.

She spent summer, fall, winter, spring in a poorly insulated
stand,
no toys, cheap food, life on a fifteen-foot chain
waiting for someone to love her.

When I came out to visit
she jumped on me,
and because I was too young
to understand the desperation of loneliness,
I left her.

My father lost the right to see his children,
and when my mother got full custody,
Patches stayed chained to her doghouse.

Years later, I found out
the one time she was let inside
she ate rat poison and died.

This is how I learned to care for dogs.

This is why when the time comes
and I find an outside dog
who might enjoy the inside,
I open the door.

On How Dogs Choose Their People

The day he proclaims,
I want a dog, too,
I shrug and say, *Okay.*

When he brings her to meet me,
I stop mid-step, taken by
the soft chocolate of her fur.
She's beautiful, I whisper,
and she licks me.

In the days that follow,
she finds herself on my bed,
follows my dog and me to the bathroom,
lays outside the door and waits.

He seeths,
She is supposed to be my dog,
and yet, she has picked me,
because trauma recognizes trauma
        and seeks it out.

When he takes my money,
my prescribed painkillers,
and his stuff,
I tell him to leave the dog.

When the vet consoles me, saying,
She was sick before she was yours,
All I hear is
        She was yours.

They Told Me

She will bite you as you sleep,
she will kill your other dogs,
she can't be trusted around children.

You should put her down before she hurts someone,
you cannot trust her near cats,
you're too small to control a dog like that.

Insurance companies will refuse her,
or charge extra if I identify what she is.

Landlords will refuse to rent,
unless my therapist offers Emotion Support Animal
documentation.

They did not tell me we would fall in love,
that she would sleep on the bed every single night,
greet me at the door with a tennis ball each day.

They did not see the day a four-year-old came over,
pulled on her ears,
and stepped on her tail
and she let him.

They only ever saw
that she was a pit bull.

An Apology to Kyla

You were always second best
came into the picture after I'd already found the love
that would surpass them all,
earned scars on your ears to prove you exist,
fought for your place on the bed,
resting on the pillow,
snoring, facing me.

You tried to get me to notice you,
so much so,
you got sick first,
mapping out cancer care
before he could succumb.

And by the time he died,
you grieved so deeply,
both of us losing our best friend,
we couldn't be around each other.
You slept on the blankets he used to rest on for months.

And by the time you got sicker,
I was still grieving for him,
to appreciate you.

The Weight of a Dog

Baxter weighed one hundred and thirty pounds,
Kyla weighs sixty-five pounds,
Zoë weighs fifty-one pounds,
and Enyo weighs forty.

In an emergency, I can lift them,
carry them, back to the apartment
into the car if needed.

I weigh one hundred and thirty pounds.
Kyla is half my weight.

She is elderly, grey face and cloudy eyes,
Cushings disease, two types of cancer,
history of heart worm,
ruptured ear drum and more.

When Baxter got sick,
I worked overtime in another state to afford his chemo.
When Kyla got sick,
I drove once a month to the vet for her meds,
scoured every inch of her body for any abnormalities.

My mother used to tell me
during the war my dziadek
got stranded during a battle,
no food, no water.

And though he befriended a stray dog
before he could starve to death,
he killed and ate it.

Now I read stories of the family in Ukraine
whose bodies litter the street
alongside their two dogs.

I read stories of the family who carried
their elderly German Shepard for kilometers
until they crossed the borders
though they could have been just like the other family.

If the bombs went off here,
I would break my legs
if it meant bringing them to safety.

Sun Naps

After the next surgery,
where insides come out to be tested,
where nipples are removed and replaced with scar tissue,
she says she wants to go outside.

The sun is blocked by wildfire smoke,
but the sun still pushes through the bleak,
still warms the earth here without igniting it.

We stand for a time until her back legs tire,
and she lays outside of the shade of the tree.
In direct sunlight until she becomes so warm
she feels like she can burst.

And here,
she is happy as she falls asleep.
We stay as long as she wants.

When He Screams Long Enough A Local Domestic Abuse Survivor Gets Text Reading, "Are You Safe?"

The night he wants to talk about our relationship, I caution maybe in the morning, maybe not right now. He pushes, and I relent, a volcano out of my mouth finally saying, *I've been struggling for weeks to figure out how to end this.*

He looks like I've stabbed him with the dog leash I'm holding, face color peeling like the drywall in our—my—apartment from rain damage. *But,* he says, *I don't want to live without you.* I shrug, *That's no longer your decision.*

My pitbull senses the lightning in the air, and moves closer to me. I take the leash from his hands, so I can keep both dogs safe. He advances, finger a familiar arrow and I see the way my father once shoved this dart against my sister's chest hard enough to leave a bullseye print.

My pitbull is also a rescue, she slams her body against me, asking *Now?* She, too, has been here before. I stroke her face in answer, *Not yet, we are okay.*

Still, her body ridges like a mountain of granite, a linebacker ready to demolish the person in her path, to bring her football safely home, and I wonder if only bad people are afraid of her breed because they've seen her defend her person from them.

I'll kill myself, he threatens between clenched teeth. And the laugh erupts out of me before I can choke it back. I have only ever heard this threat as a precipitant to the violence when a woman stays in hopes of saving his life.

That'd be your choice, I say.

Because I've made mine.

As we walk home, he screams behind us, voice echoing in the otherwise abandoned road and Kyla wags her tail.

Playtime

Today I watched my dog crumple like a piece of paper,
watched her forget her age,
rear like a lion, and her back legs
fold like a letter in an envelope.

When the puppy went after her again,
slamming into my old girl's front paws,
which then buckled with the soft grace of age,
and her body, an elderly accordion,
slowly hum to the ground.

And my old girl with her milky eyes,
lay there, startled to suddenly be on the grass,
tail wagging as if it was all part of the play,
as if aging is just a game.

The Judge

It has been some time since I've taken a moment
to look at the white dandelions spreading across her face
the cumulus clouds of her eyes.

She is slowing down each day
footing a little more unsure each step
occasional stumbles and pauses to regroup,
a small limp that unless you were looking for, you'd miss.

She is straddling this world and the next
communing with the living and dead,
moving closer to the next with each white fur that crops up.

And I am tasked with judging when
to ensure gentle passage.

In This Photo

What you can't see in this picture
is that the lump under the brown throw blanket
is the dog who can't function without being tucked in.

What you can't see in this picture
is the balled form,
snout resting on tightly coiled back paws,
tail tying it all together.

What you can't see in this picture
is the fight the girls got in two years ago,
the one where Enyo's teeth were ripped from her mouth,
and Kyla walked with a limp from a puncture through her elbow.

You can't see the scars that riddle Kyla's body,
the half-moon marks on her face,
the mass under her harness,
the pink slice across her right side,

the cancer hidden
just beneath the skin.

The Love of a Dog

When we went to Michigan to visit my family,
I would leave my dogs with my mother.

Sometimes she would call me to say
my girl hasn't left the window.
"It's like all the light had left her."

Once as a joke I asked my roommate
what Kyla loved more,
me or her tennis balls?

My roommate paused before saying,
You know, when you're gone,
she doesn't play with her toys.

How I'll Know When It's Time

I tell myself I'll know when she can't
make it the full block walk anymore,
but then again, there was that entire summer
where she took naps halfway through, so maybe not.

I tell myself I'll know when she stops finding her tennis balls,
meeting me at the door, body so full of love
it rattles like a toy,
tail knocking the coffee table clean.

I tell myself I'll know when her bowl still holds food,
when she doesn't come to the couch,
eyes desperate for just a small taste
of whatever is on my plate.

I tell myself I'll know when her head doesn't rise to greet me,
her ears stay down,
tail barely wagging,
body limp,
like she's ready for rest.

Do I Just Let The Cancer Take You?

After the aspiration for the lump I found two days ago,
the oncologist calls me to say,
"Unfortunately it does show criteria for a malignancy
and likely related to her previous diagnosis."

I cry in my office between patients,
white tissues blanketing my desk.

Two days after the call,
you wake up from a nap,
cough four times and I move fast enough
to soften the landing as your body falls to the ground.

I pet you and whisper soft words,
"It's okay, it's okay. Catch your breath.
I'm right here."

My hands run along your stomach,
and there are mountains beneath the skin,
all the way from harness to groin.

I imagine the surgery,
the slice from chest to back leg,
the bruising and healing after.

The oncologist said surgery wouldn't be the wrong option.
But she also never said it would be the right one.

An Ode to Kyla PoopiePants

Nicknames included Poops, Poops-a-loo,
Madame Poops, Poopie, etc.
She was a seventy-five pound
poop colored pit bull,
whose tail was more whip than wag.

I never thought feces would determine
so much of my life for nine years, but—
I knew I wanted to date a guy
when she rubbed her poopie butt on his hoodie
and it smeared across his chest.
I braced for him to yell,
or push her away.

But he just sat there and asked for napkins.

When she was diagnosed with Cushings disease,
I found the people worthwhile
were the ones willing to still cuddle with her
at the risk of getting leaked on.

Once, Kyla pooped five times in a single block walk.
Another time, though we'd just let her outside,
she made eye contact with us, and pooped on the floor.
At a conference Boston one year,
it was the fanciest hotel we had ever been in.
Upon arrival we were yelling, "No, Kyla!
Don't you dare!" as we raced our girl,
squatting in the hallway, to the elevator.

Once, a friend gave me their old couch,
and while I was outside thanking him,
no longer than five minutes,
Madame Poops shit on the cushions.

If anything, her nicknames fit her and
it's how I knew we were home.

Still Life In A Capitalist Nightmare

The therapist is ugly crying on the floor,
with her dog's body twisting in front of her,
neck arched so far backward she fears it may
break itself.

The dog's urine sprays like a hose
amid convulsions on the carpet.

The therapist screams *Help!* to her roommate,
who yells back, *What do you want?*
and she sobs, *Kyla is having a seizure, get towels.*

The therapist strokes the brown dog's fur
and tells her *it's okay,*
it's alright.

As Kyla comes to, she rests her head in her person's hands,
as though her person is the only light that guided her through,
and the therapist cries harder.

There is no sick-time left.
No PTO accrual.

So in ten minutes,
I am supposed to dry my eyes,
return to my office,
and welcome the next patient
with a smile.

I Have Not Slept Since The Seizure

She lays in bed with me
and I twist my spine hamburger instead of hot dog
so as to not disturb where she plops down.

In grad school they called it the reptilian brain,
the part of us that we inherited from cavemen,
what keeps us breathing,
our heart pounding,

our brain scanning for threat
even while we sleep.
Strange now how the threat resides in her body,
a simple cough that causes spasm,
spasm that causes seizure.

I wake if her breathing changes.
I wake if she runs in her sleep.
I wake if nothing has happened.

Because the threat shares this bed with us,
its cold fingers expanding with each second.
And the shadow silently spreading across her body,
will take her from me.

Kyla

My mother watches my girl
unfurl from the couch and move haphazardly
to the bedroom.

She's slowing down, my mother comments, eyes thick
with store bought sadness.

It's true—
her once lively step is halted,
the fur that frames her face is grey and white.
her eyes have become milky pools.

She is slowing down, I say.
But I have had to let go of a dog
whose life gave out before
his body.

And this—watching her age—watching
her slow, taking more measured steps,
having to help her on the couch, into bed, in the car as
she can no longer twist her hips
to jostle her forward.

This I tell my mother, *This isn't sad, this is a gift, a privilege.*
Getting to watch her go from mountain hiking, tennis ball
chasing youth,
to aged walks more pee breaks to the eventual still.

Reality

The reality is this,
even before the re-diagnosis,
I was amazed she made it this far—
one paw slowly losing the ability to bear weight,
the way she stopped reacting to dogs as we passed,
moments she tried to jump on the bed
only to fall like a tennis ball to the carpet,
the days her gums were as white as a rawhide.

Last year around this time,
I told people I would be shocked
if she made it to the new year.

But she did,
and now we're six months in.

The truth is this isn't the first collapse,
the fifth collapse,
and we can't figure out why they're happening.

The truth is,
I know she's dying.

I'm just not ready.

Decline

Let me tell you about the way a body twists when it's sick—
How the muscle wastes away
and all that is left is hip bones and spine.

Let me tell you about legs that shake
labored breaths
and a swollen stomach.

Let me tell you about restless sleep
a neck that jerks back so quickly
you'd think it could snap.

Let me tell you about legs buckling on the stairs
and the full pitch forward,
last stair catching and twisting what remains.

Let me tell you about knowing the end is coming,
and still giving medication
like there is any semblance of hope left.

A Bad Night

My roommate and I lay in bed
an hour before the alarm is scheduled to go off.
He says, *She's having a bad night,*
and I tell him I've been up for hours.

She'd had a bad night two nights before, too.
When I told my roommate,
he'd asked if I was just drunk.

We lay in silence listening to her struggle for breath,
taking turns petting her head, offering comfort,
and telling her she's okay.

He whispers, *You know,*
it's not the wrong time to call it,
and I tell him not yet,
not yet.

An Ode to My Roommate

After the emergency vet for the seizure that doesn't stop,
my roommate takes her to one of her regular vets to follow up.
Before he goes, he asks me what to tell them.
I say to add more medication.

When they ask him to do blood work,
he says no.
When they ask him to do imaging,
he says no.

Though I tell him he can put me on speaker phone,
he does not consult me.

I am angry with him for weeks
until we have to rush her in again
until we have to do the imaging
and have to do the blood work.

The vet says
 "I want to show you her x-ray."
And I tell her,
"I hate this already."

Because the truth is,
if my roommate had done it then,
we'd have found out what we know now,
and given up much sooner.

What The End Looks Like

The end is a black and white screen
with your dog's body splayed out.

Look at the spine and wonder if it's shifted.
Look at the organs and bones you recognize, and the ones
you don't.

The vet will circle "This right here?"
and "And then this one."

The end looks like two well-formed masses
as you're already losing your dog to cancer.

One in her chest,
the other on her spleen.

The end looks like a bloody nose
and fluid in her lungs that rattles like a broken squeak toy.

The end is you on the floor,
with your dog's paw in your hand whispering,
"I love you, I love you, I love you."

This Isn't Goodbye, This Is See You Soon

Remember when we used to hike?

How you would run so far ahead
stop and wait impatiently for me to catch up
before sprinting off again?

Remember how you could maintain this
for seven miles or more?

Remember how you weren't afraid to run up ahead
because you knew I'd be right behind you?

This is just like that.

Go on up ahead, girl.

I'll be right behind you.

A Field Guide To Removing Your Dead Dog's Harness

Step One:
You will not stop crying.

Step Two:
Ask the veterinarian if it's okay. Yes, this was your dog, and yes it is your harness, but you might feel like you need permission for what to do next.

Step Three:
Rest your hand near the clasp. Notice how still the body is. How the head doesn't turn, the tail doesn't wag.

Step Four:
Push until it undoes.

Step Five:
Slide it gently down the paws, as though the body is now as fragile as the stick they used to chew on. Don't break a bone, don't disturb the rest.

Step Six:
Pull the harness to your chest searching for the last fragments of warmth.

Step Seven:
When this too turns cold, stand up, brush your pants off. Ask the staff to be gentle with the body when they move it, when they pass it to the next person to cremate it.

Step Eight:
Offer one final pat, kiss on the head, I love you, and thank you for being my friend to the lifeless body on the floor.

Step Nine:
Walk out, empty harness and leash dangling by your side.

Step Ten:
Make sure your car door is closed before you scream.

Step Eleven:
Repeat for every dog you will ever own.

Cremation

After they are dead I consider asking
the doctors if they could cut it out,
if they could slice open the abdomen,
scoop it out as though it is ice cream,
and preserve it in a jar for me.

I would put the jar on the shelf at home,
or perhaps in my office at work.
I would smile at it with my canines pointed,
tell it - you may have killed them,
but I killed you.

Sporadically, I would shake the jar,
watch it suspended in a yellow ocean wave,
watch the way it crumbles,
the way small fragments separate from the whole.

Its ashes would never be spread on a mountain top,
at a favorite beach.
If I asked the doctors to cut it out,
it would never get the honor of decaying.

If I asked them to cut it out,
when they cremated them,
I wouldn't have to live with the knowledge
that even after death,
their cancer is still with them.

Not Ready to Let Go

I carry my dead dogs for months.
They come to work with me,
stay buckled into the passenger seat
while I meet with clients.
When I work on contact notes,
they sit atop my desk,
the way they used to lay on their beds.
I'm careful to face the window so they can look out,
or so that they can look in.
I carry them on the bad days,
hands touching the cool wood box,
grasping for some trace of warmth.
I carry them on the road trips
because they hated being left home.
I carry them, carry them, carry them,
because I'm not ready to let go.

For Those Who Say Animals Don't Have Souls

I wish you tail wags,
and paws that reach out for pets.

I wish you a snoring head on your pillow at night,
and small asks to get under the blankets.

I wish you sun naps on Fall days,
leashes, and campfires.

I wish you face kisses when you are sad,
and car rides with windows cracked.

I wish you a companion that you fully fall in love with,
and money spent on toys, and jackets, and soft beds.

I wish you your heart shattering
when you hear the voicemail because the cancer has
returned.

I wish you devastation because by your belief,
you won't be reunited.

Alternate Universe Where Your Death Is More Gentle

In this poem, the money does not run out.
I am not forced to find a job,
not trying to save up money.
I can stay home.
I have time to notice the lump
before it becomes marble sized.
Before the spider web of cancer builds a nest
and spreads like spilled milk.

In this poem, we can do the surgery.
The vet is competent and we find the right meds
so it's safe to be on chemo.

In this poem, we start the chemo sooner.
I do not flinch when they say
it costs nearly $800 a month.
The cancer does not spread through your chest,
create fluid in your lungs.

In this poem, you still die.
But I do not have to leave work early.
I do not scream in my car as I drive home.
You do not bleed into my hands
while my roommate speeds to the clinic.

Instead, you are just tired.
One night, maybe a year or two from now,
I help you into bed.
You curl up beside me.
We fall asleep together.
And in the morning,
you don't wake up.

Dear Stranger,

You don't know me, but I have loved your dog for the last nine years.

I want you to know the first month I had her she ate my belt. And as I stood over her, angry and frustrated, she shook in fear before tucking her head so that if I hit her, her face wouldn't be hurt. In that moment, I told her she could crap wherever she wanted. She could eat whatever she wanted. But moving forward, she was safe with me.

A few years later, she ate my fanciest pair of boots. When I held them up to ask "Who did this?" she proceeded to wag her tail, take them from my hands, and continue happily chewing. She healed enough to trust me not to hurt her.

Without her, I wouldn't have gone to grad school. Sarah and Baxter died two weeks before school started. And Eben died the Friday before my final class. My last day was the same day as his funeral. Some of my professors allowed her into classes and trainings. If not for her comfort, I couldn't have done it. She started with me, and she walked out of the building on our last day.

She became an old lady dog—not only slowed down, but grey face and eyes that pooled more milk by the day. By the end, she had three types of cancer, and Cushing's disease. Her body was tired, and I knew she'd leave me soon.

We did a bucket list: one last mountain top view at Sunday River, one last kayaking trip, one last poetry reading at Topsham Library.

There were more things to do, but the day my roommate called while I was at work to say she had a bloody nose, and I knew. I screamed the whole way home before we drove her to the vet.

I thought you'd want to know, her final meal—
        a pup cup from Starbucks,
        Arby's roast beef sliders,
        and junk snacks I otherwise never let her eat.

As she fell asleep, I held her paw and stroked her fur.

She knew she was loved, and she was ready to go.

I guess all of this is to say –

        Dear Stranger,
        I adopted your dog.
        I loved her as long as I could.
        And I will miss her forever.

An Ode To The Now Vs Then Rescue Dog Photo

The day you come home with me,
you cower, tucking yourself so small,
I bite back tears and tell you,
I'm so sorry for what happened.

When I kneel down
like a prayer, soft and gentle,
offering the palms of my hands,
you slowly come to me.

I am cautious, careful to move
at a fraction of the speed I would move
with my dogs.

The first month,
you run from people on our walkies.
You don't know how to play with toys,
how to sleep on a bed.

When we give you a bath,
the grime and dirt flows down the drain,
covering the white bathtub,
coloring like a book.

The first time you approach a stranger to say hi,
I nearly sob because you trust,
somehow, I will keep you safe.

When I come home,
you jump into my arms now.
When we go to bed at night,
your face rests beside mine on the pillow.

Lynne Schmidt is the queer, neurodivergent grandchild of a Holocaust survivor, and a mental health professional with a focus in trauma and healing. Lynne is a 2025 Maine Arts Fellow. They are the winner of the 2021 The Poetry Question Chapbook Contest for their chapbook, *Sexy Time*, & 2020 New Women's Voices Contest for their chapbook, *Dead Dog Poems*. Lynne is also the author of the chapbooks, *Dying Dog Poems, The Unaccounted For Circles Of Hell*, and *Gravity*, which has been listed as one of the 100 Best Breakup Books Of All Time by Book Authority. When given the choice, Lynne prefers the company of her pack of dogs and one cat to humans.